BOOKS AND GUIDES

WEDDLE's Guide to Employment Sites on the Internet

"Restaurant patrons looking for quality dining have Zagat to guide their cuisine needs. For the recruitment industry, the name is Weddle ... Peter Weddle that is."
American Staffing Association

"I've known Peter Weddle for years. He is an immensely likeable guy. He is also extremely knowledgeable. Highly recommended!"
Richard Nelson Bolles, What Color is Your Parachute?

"A wealth of updated and useful information."
Library Journal

"WEDDLE's is a very useful tool that recruiters and HR professionals will find helpful."
Fortune Magazine

"When in doubt, consider WEDDLE's ... an industry standard."
HR WIRE

"If you're looking for an objective guide to employment Web-sites, ExecuNet recommends WEDDLE's Guide.
ExecuNet Center for Executive Careers

Work Strong: Your Personal Career Fitness System

"Peter Weddle's Career Fitness System empowers you to take your job search to the next level and achieve lasting career success."

Diana Miller, CEO Community Job Club

"There are few people in the world who are as passionate about our careers and our own unique talents as Peter Weddle. Work Strong changes the paradigms of career management books and is sure to give you a new perspective on how to Work Strong in your own career."

Aaron Matos, CEO Jobing

"This book is a guide to finding yourself and to charting a new course for a 21st Century career. A must read!"

Kevin Wheeler, CEO Global Learning Resources, Inc.

"A lifetime of career happiness in a single book!"

Dan Honig, WorkplaceDiversity.com

In today's world, it's not enough to work hard. You also have to work strong and perform at your peak. That's the power and promise of this book."

John Bell, CEO Boxwood Technology

Generalship: HR Leadership in a Time of War

"... a wake-up call for those of us in HR. We need to take on the accountability for effecting change. ... This book provides a great strategy for doing just that."

Regina DeTore, VP/HR Sepracor, Inc.

"... a must-read book for human resource professionals, especially those who seek to be true leaders in their corporation."

Jerome N. Carter, SVP/HR International Paper

"Human Resources is now facing extraordinary challenges. This demanding time requires the kind of bold, thoughtful and thorough leadership suggested by this book."

Guy Patton, EVP/HR Fidelity Investments

"Don't miss this book. It's Machiavelli's *The Prince* and Covey's *7 Habits of Highly Effective People* all rolled into one for the HR profession."

Donna Introcaso, VP/HR iVillage

"This book is a must-read on HR leadership, not only for HR practitioners, but for every CEO and Company Director, as well.

Robert S. Nadel, President Nadel Consulting

Recognizing Richard Rabbit: A Fable About Being True to Yourself

"A magical way to explore the essence of you."
Jennifer Floren, CEO Experience

"... a very intriguing and unique book."
Patrick Erwin, The Work Buzz CareerBuilder.com

"... if you're thinking about making changes in your personal life or want a pep talk about being true to yourself, check out this book."
Celeste Blackburn, Managing Editor Resources for Humans

"The story inspires useful reflection and a practical rethinking of your own personal effectiveness in work and life."
Jonathan Goodman, Review on Social Median

Career Fitness: How to Find, Win & Keep the Job You Want in the 1990s

"This book is phenomenal! It'll help you run the race of your life at work each day."
Harvey McKay, Swim With the Sharks Without Being Eaten Alive

"... street-smart wisdom, coupled with practical career workout tools ... sure to be useful to people at any point in their career."
Madelyn Jennings, SVP/HR Gannett Company, Inc.

WEDDLE'S BOOKS & GUIDES FOR EMPLOYERS & RECRUITERS

The Talent Recruiting and Sourcing Handbook: Source better, smarter, faster, and cheaper than the competition, Shally Steckerl (Spring, 2013)

The A+ Solution: How America's Professional Societies and Trade Associations Can Solve the Nation's Workforce Skills Crisis, John Bell & Christine Smith (Spring 2013)

Finding Needles in a Haystack: Keywords for Finding Top Talent in Resume Databases, Wendy S. Enelow

Generalship: HR Leadership in a Time of War, Peter Weddle

The Keys to Successful Recruiting and Staffing, Barry Siegel

Postcards from Space: Being the Best in Online Recruitment & HR Management, Peter Weddle

WEDDLE's Guide to Employment Sites on the Internet, Peter Weddle

WEDDLE's Guide to Association Web Sites, Peter Weddle

WEDDLE'S Guide to Staffing Firms & Employment Agencies, Peter Weddle

Available at amazon.com and Weddles.com

WEDDLE'S BOOKS & GUIDES FOR JOB SEEKERS & CAREER ACTIVISTS

The Career Fitness Workbook: How to Find, Win & Hang Onto the Job of Your Dreams, Peter Weddle

A Multitude of Hope: A Novel About Rediscovering the American Dream, Peter Weddle

The Success Matrix: Wisdom from the Web on How to Get Hired & Not Be Fired, Peter Weddle

Job Nation: The 100 Best Employment Sites on the Web, Peter Weddle

The Career Activist Republic, Peter Weddle

Work Strong: Your Personal Career Fitness System, Peter Weddle

Recognizing Richard Rabbit: A Fable About Being True to Yourself, Peter Weddle

Career Fitness: How to Find, Win & Keep the Job You Want in the 1990's, Peter Weddle

WEDDLE's Guide to Employment Sites on the Internet, Peter Weddle

WEDDLE's Guide to Association Web Sites, Peter Weddle

WEDDLE'S Guide to Staffing Firms & Employment Agencies, Peter Weddle

The New Golden Rules of Job Board Success

FOUR PRINCIPLES FOR
OPTIMIZING OPERATIONAL AND
BOTTOM LINE PERFORMANCE
IN THE 21ST CENTURY

Peter Weddle

WEDDLE's Books are available in bulk through Independent Publishers Group, 814 North Franklin Street, Chicago, IL 60610, ph: 312-337-0747, www.ipgbook.com. Individual copies may be purchased at amazon.com and Weddles.com.

ISBN: 978-1-928734-81-9

Copyright © 2013 by Peter Weddle.

This publication may not be reproduced, stored in a retrieval system or transmitted, in whole or part, in any form or by any means, electronic, mechanical, photocopying, recording or otherwise, without the prior written permission of WEDDLE's LLC, 2052 Shippan Avenue, Stamford, CT 06902.

TABLE OF CONTENTS

Introduction	13
Please Read This Page First	17
What Are the New Golden Rules?	19
The Golden Rule of Traffic Development What you do to attract the best talent will also attract mediocre talent, but the converse is not true.	21
The Golden Rule of Market Positioning Purity may make philosophers smile, but it turns off paying customers.	43
The Golden Rule of Customer Cultivation An educated recruiter is your best customer, and an educated job board is the best teacher.	67
The Golden Rule of Customer Satisfaction One trick ponies may thrive in the circus, but they're doomed to extinction in the marketplace.	95
About the International Association of Employment Web Sites (IAEWS)	113
WEDDLE's Syndicated Content for Job Boards	115
About the Author	117

Introduction

In 1991, I launched a company called Job Bank USA. Five years later, I sold it to a division of Spherion and set out to pursue a career in writing. As luck would have it, at that very same moment, Dow Jones was searching for someone to write about these new destinations on the Internet called "job boards." And so began a love affair with an industry that has, for more than two decades, revolutionized the way people and organizations find one another in the world of work.

First for *National Business Employment Weekly* and later for the interactive edition of *The Wall Street Journal*, I had the privilege of watching job boards define, create and bring to maturity the online employment services industry. I looked on as they developed ever better technology and ever more helpful services for job seekers and employers alike. And, I was there to witness the huge successes and the occasional crashes that have been the chapter headings of their history.

Along the way, I talked to the dreamers who sketched out the industry's foundation on countless napkins and to the builders who laid the bricks and mortar of its superstructure. I met the big personalities and the driven entrepreneurs, the quirky technologists and the consummate salespeople who populated this new frontier. And, I got to write about all of it. I was the proverbial kid in the candy store.

Those dispatches and my memories form the foundation of this book. *The New Golden Rules of Job Board Success* does not, however, present conventional wisdom. It doesn't restate maxims and assumptions that are generally known and accepted in the industry today. Instead, the book consciously challenges what many job boards consider fundamental precepts. Why? Because its purpose is to define the pathway to job board success in the 21st century, not the 20th, in the present and the future, not the past.

Finally, as every author notes, while this book draws on the wisdom of many, it is my creation, and I bear sole responsibility for what you will read. That said, if you are engaged in the management or operation of a job board or in any way connected to the online employment services industry, I hope you will find the principles presented here useful or, at the very least, thought provoking.

    Peter Weddle
    Stamford, Connecticut
    USA

PETER WEDDLE

Please Read This Page First

Unfortunately, we live in a world of papier-mâché ethics. Inevitably, therefore, some will get a hold of this book – especially those with an axe to grind or a bias to feed – and misuse it. They will take comments out of context and use them to bash job boards. They'll say, "Aha, here's a guy who has long supported job boards and look at the things he's saying."

So, let me assert right up front, the opinions I express and the data I offer in this book are NOT, implicitly or explicitly, a condemnation or even a criticism of job boards. Quite the contrary, they are both a celebration of their service to employers, recruiters, job seekers and career activists and a roadmap for their continued and even expanded role in supporting them. The reason there are Golden Rules for job board success in the 21st century is because they have already done so much for so many people around the world in the 20th century. And because they have the potential to do so much more ... today, tomorrow and into the future.

What Are the New Golden Rules?

The new golden rules for job boards are a set of axioms that define key principles and practices that must now be applied over and above the basic blocking and tackling required to run an effective organization.

These guidelines are not a substitute for designing and delivering superior products and services or for effective sales and marketing, operations and administration, financial management, customer service and leadership. They are, instead, the steps an online employment services enterprise should take in addition to those more conventional activities, whether it is a global corporation or run by a not-for-profit association; a stand-alone venture or the subsidiary of a larger media company; a niche site or one that covers all professions, crafts and trades; a huge job board with millions of visitors or a much smaller destination with much less traffic.

Why are the new golden rules important?

Because good blocking and tackling are essential but insufficient for success in the highly competitive global and domestic markets of the 21st century. In effect, these axioms are the actions that will now spell the difference between the also-rans and the elites of the online employment services industry. The new golden rules are – to paraphrase another axiom – the rules that determine who gets the gold in the 21st century employment services marketplace.

The Golden Rule of Traffic Development

What you do to attract the best talent will also attract mediocre talent, but the converse is not true.

Job boards are not self-contained or stand-alone entities. They are part of the larger employment marketplace in virtually every geographic location, occupation and industry. And, all marketplaces operate according to a fixed truth: they can either evolve or they can wither away. They can either adapt to changing circumstances or they can become irrelevant. There are no other choices.

As their name implies, job boards were originally created as an online platform where employers could advertise their open jobs and active job seekers could apply for them. Unlike newspapers, however, the jobs posted on a job board were visible for more than a single day and were not confined to the limited and therefore expensive real estate of the printed page. They were easier to find, more informative and more applicant-friendly than traditional classified ads.

As a consequence, in the space of less than a decade, job boards went from a quirky, new technological innovation to the primary means of both recruitment for employers and job search for those in transition.

By 2007, for example, the CareerXroads 7th Annual Source of Hire Survey found that job boards were the second greatest source of external hires for large employers (i.e., new employees hired from outside the organization), trailing only referrals and only by less than three percentage points. In that year, they accounted for 25.68 percent of all external hires – more than open houses, search engines, career fairs, agencies, campus recruiting and print advertising combined.

WEDDLE's Source of Employment Survey, in contrast, examined the preferences of both employers and job seekers and thus had a much larger survey population, yet it yielded similar results. In 2007, it found that:

- Job boards were the #1 sourcing strategy employers used to acquire top quality candidates. It was selected by an astonishing 51.66 percent of large, medium and small employers – more than posting jobs on their own Web-sites, career fairs, the use of staffing firms, social networking sites, and search engine marketing combined.

- Job boards were also the #1 way job seekers found their last job and the #1 way they expected to find their next job. Over one-in-five (20.2 percent) of the more than 15,000 respondents said they found their last job using a job board, easily outdistancing the second highest response – a tip from a friend – which captured just 7.4 percent of the responses.

Even more impressive, over a quarter of those same respondents (27.3 percent) thought that job boards would be the source of their next job, with the second highest response – sending their resume into a company the old fashioned way – getting the nod from just 6.2 percent of the respondents.

...in the space of less than a decade, job boards went from a quirky, new technological innovation to the primary means of both recruitment for employers and job search for those in transition.

Five years later and despite a Great Recession and the rise of social media in the employment space on the Web, the results from WEDDLE's 2012 Survey gave an even more resounding vote of support to job boards. Over half of all employer and recruiter respondents (56.9 percent) said that posting a job on a commercial job board "provides the best quality applicants." The second highest response – posting jobs on their own corporate site – was selected by just 13.7 percent of the respondents. And despite all the brouhaha about LinkedIn, Twitter and Facebook, using a social networking site drew less than 2 percent of the votes from employers.

The results from working men and women were just as positive. These individuals represented a good cross-section of the workforce:

- 22.4 percent were executives
- 20.5 percent were mid-level professionals
- 17.6 percent were managers
- 17.4 percent were senior-level professionals
- 8.1 percent were entry-level professionals
- 5.9 percent were skilled tradespeople
- 8.1 percent listed themselves some other category.

Almost half (47.2 percent) of these respondents were employed but either thinking about or actively searching for a new position. Fewer than four-in-ten (38.4 percent) were unemployed and actively in transition. And, the remainder described themselves in some other way.

As shown in the chart on the next page, these respondents had been well served by job boards.

Better than one-third (33.9 percent) said they found their last job at a job board. The second highest response was again a tip from a friend, which was selected by 11.5 percent of the respondents. Just 3.2 percent said a social networking site had been the source of their employment.

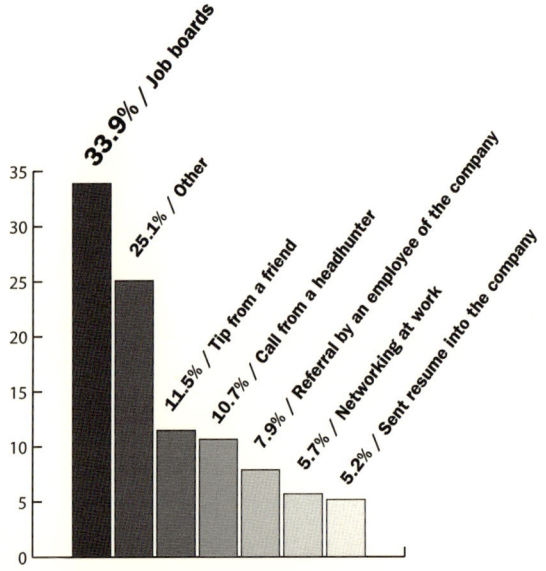

Job Seekers' Source of Last Employment

How does that 33.9 percent record of people who found a job at a job board stack up against other areas of human endeavor? It's better than the batting average of baseball Hall of Famers Hank Aaron (.305) and Yogi Berra (.285). It's better than the scoring percentage of the best strikers in world soccer, Felipe Caicedo (.333) and Milivoje Novakovic (.316). And, to return to the "business" arena, it is greater than the winning percentage of the cat token selected in an online ballot to replace the iron in the game of Monopoly (31.0 percent).

The expectations around the future performance of job boards were even higher. When, respondents were asked how they thought they would find their next job, over half (54.9 percent) indicated a job board. The second highest response – getting a call from a headhunter – was selected by just 7.7 percent of those in the survey. And, social media? Just 4.1 percent of the respondents thought they would find their next job at a social networking site.

A summary of their responses is presented in the following chart. They do not total to 100 percent because not all of the possible choices are shown.

Job Seekers' Source of Next Employment

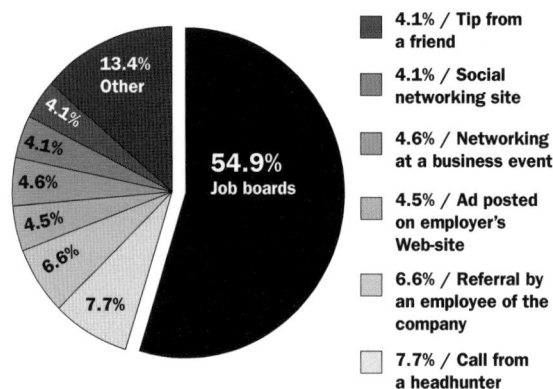

- 4.1% / Tip from a friend
- 4.1% / Social networking site
- 4.6% / Networking at a business event
- 4.5% / Ad posted on employer's Web-site
- 6.6% / Referral by an employee of the company
- 7.7% / Call from a headhunter
- 54.9% Job boards
- 13.4% Other

The Rise of Corporate Classifieds

Even as employers were becoming more comfortable with using job boards, however, they began to see an advantage in doing their own online hosting of job announcements. As a consequence, more and more employers began to develop "career" or "employment" areas on their corporate Web-sites. Originally limited to major enterprises, these "corporate classifieds" now appear on the sites of medium-sized and even small employers. With widely varying degrees of detail and sophistication, they are used to post an employer's open jobs and describe its culture, benefits and other aspects of employment.

In their earliest incarnation, these corporate classifieds struggled to attract job seekers. Because the career or employment area on most corporate Websites was controlled by the corporate IT Department, it was seldom well designed for recruitment, often had an uninspiring appearance and frequently offered rudimentary functionality. Worse, it had to compete with commercial job boards, which were spending millions of dollars to attract job seekers, develop eye catching designs and provide a job search experience – by listing opportunities from multiple organizations – that was more productive than that provided by a single employer's site. Indeed, the situation grew so dire that in 2005, the Internet Corporation for Assigned Names & Numbers (ICANN) authorized the creation of a special top level domain called .JOBS (dot JOBS) which employers could purchase to help them attract job seekers to the open positions posted on their own Web-sites.

Even as .JOBS was launched, however, it was overtaken by events in the workforce. Employers discovered that job seekers had become so proficient at finding their sites and the job posted there that they no longer needed a simplistic naming crutch to attract them. In fact, as the Great Recession of 2008 threw more and more people into the job market, employers found their resume databases filled to overflowing with applications. Instead of having too few candidates visiting their sites, they increasingly had too many. And yet, the caliber of these job seekers was not what many employers needed.

The Quality Conundrum

Recruiters typically categorize workers as either active or passive job seekers.

- Active job seekers are almost always unemployed. They need a new job so usually take the initiative to search for one. They have the time and are motivated to make the effort to visit individual employer sites and view the jobs that are posted there. As a result, they represent the vast majority of the visitors to corporate classifieds.

- Passive job seekers, on the other hand, are normally employed. While they don't need a new job, they are often interested in finding a better one. Because they have a job, however, they have something to lose and thus are both cautious in their search and much more fickle when considering alternative employment opportunities. As a result, they seldom visit corporate classifieds.

This situation creates two problems for employers.

First, it forces them to recruit in a very small segment of the working population. In the United States, for example, the U.S. Bureau of Labor Statistics reports that, at any given time, just 16 percent of the workforce is actively looking for a job. In other words, over four-fifths of all workers are NOT active job seekers. They are not even passive job seekers. By definition, they are, at best, passive prospects.

Active Job Seekers & Passive Prospects in the U.S.

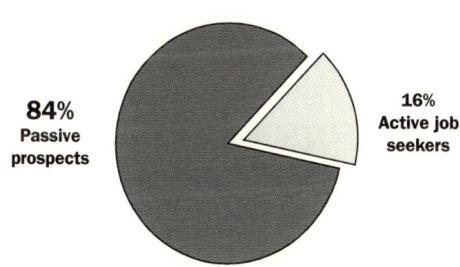

84% Passive prospects

16% Active job seekers

A similar situation undoubtedly exists in Canada, Great Britain, and the countries of the European Union, the Asia-Pacific region and South America.

Despite the uneven global economy and troubles in some sectors of the euro zone, the reality is that most workers in most countries are employed and thus not actively looking for a job. For that reason, they are unlikely to invest the time or make the effort to visit an employer's corporate classifieds.

Second, this constricted flow of visitors also undermines the quality of the yield employers generate from their corporate classifieds. While almost all recruiters will say that they consider active job seekers just as potentially qualified for their openings as passive prospects, they are much less inclusive in practice. Indeed, when presented with two equally qualified candidates, one of whom is unemployed and actively looking for a job and the other who is employed and thus inactive, they will almost always select the passive prospect. Why? Because, unconsciously or otherwise, they believe the employed person is likely to be the better performer.

In addition, the math works against them. The much larger size of the passive population means that there are inevitably more high performers in that group than in the smaller cohort of active job seekers. With corporate classifieds only able to attract the active population, however, employers can't reach that talent with their site.

For example, if 5 percent of 1,000 workers or 50 people perform at a superior level, an employer will only be able to compete for 8 of those individuals with its corporate classifieds (the 16 percent of the 50 top performers who are actively seeking a new job). The other 42 workers (the 84 percent of the 50 top performers who are passive prospects) would have to be recruited some other way.

What does this quality conundrum mean for job boards? Simply this: employers no longer need job boards to connect them with active job seekers. They are doing that with their own corporate classifieds. What they now need job boards to do is help them reach 100 percent of the workforce, but especially the 84 percent who are passive prospects. They need job boards to bring them the quality talent they can't access with their own sites.

Building Traffic Among Passive Prospects

Since their first appearance in the 1990s, job boards have largely limited the content they offer to job seekers to information about the principles and practices of effective job search. Typically, sites have addressed such topics as effective resume writing, interviewing and, occasionally networking and salary negotiation, but very little else. This content is, of course, clearly helpful to active job seekers. For passive prospects, however, it is neither interesting nor relevant to the way they see themselves in the workplace.

Why? Because the vast majority of passive prospects don't consider themselves job seekers, even when they are in transition. Unlike their active counterparts, they're in no rush to make a change. They have choices, one of which is to stay right where they are with their current employer. So, they don't need to look for a job, and they simply aren't interested in the rudiments of conventional job search.

They are, on the other hand, almost always interested in advancing their career. That advancement could involve taking a new job with a different employer, but just as often and maybe even more, it concerns some other aspect of good career self-management. It might, for example, involve remediation strategies for a work skill that they've not yet fully mastered or a way to deal with a supervisor who is biased in their assignment of work.

Career self-management involves both the principles and practices of being a good steward of the one-third of a person's life they will spend at work. It is based on a body of knowledge and set of skills that are just as integral and important to success as one's expertise and performance in their profession, craft or trade. It encompasses the personal setting of appropriate employment goals and the execution of specific actions to achieve them so as to provide a person with a meaningful and rewarding work experience throughout the entirety of their career.

...the vast majority of passive prospects don't consider themselves job seekers, even when they are in transition.

Career self-management isn't a nice-to-have competence; it is a critically important capability, especially in the turbulent workplace of the 21st century. Sadly, however, most workers lack even an awareness of its existence, let alone a proficiency in its application.

There are two reasons for this void:

- First, for years, workers relied on their employers to manage their careers for them. They could count on those organizations to provide a career ladder and enough job security to get them a gold watch. Today, they can't. Employers have downsized their HR Departments and eliminated that support. In the 21st century world of work, individuals are on their own. They have to manage their own careers, yet no one has given them the skills and knowledge they need to do so.

- Second, colleges and universities have turned the vast majority of their graduates into "career idiot savants." They've given their students a wealth of knowledge about this or that field of study, but taught them absolutely nothing about how to make a career in those fields. Why? Because the faculties in academia don't consider the career self-management body of knowledge and set of skills to be rigorous enough to include in the curriculum. They've left their graduates book smart and workplace ignorant.

The best way for job boards to attract and retain the allegiance of passive prospects, therefore, is to fix that problem. They should re-imagine themselves as the place where those who are employed can come to learn the skills and get the support they need to advance their own careers. Yes, that includes the rudiments of job search, but just as important, it also involves the principles and practices of effective career self-management.

Re-Imagining a Job Board

Supporting career self-management as well as job search transforms a job board from an advertising platform to a career homestead or *careerstead* – a place where people can find the content, features and functionality to advance themselves:

- when they are looking for a job

  and

- when they aren't.

It is the place to which working people turn when they're in transition AND when they're dealing with the challenges and opportunities that come along regularly throughout one's career. A careerstead does what employers used to do and what colleges and universities should have done for working men and women. It is school house, sanctuary and peer community all rolled into one.

A careerstead might provide a "career planner" feature which helps people set and update near, mid and long-term goals for their career. Or, it might include a blog where people can get answers to such questions as "how to deal with a coworker who isn't pulling their share of the load" or "what to do when confronted with an unethical situation on-the-job."

For example, though normally thought of as a job board, Monster.com offers a range of features, functionality and content to support career self-management. They include BeKnown, Monster's professional network on Facebook; discussion forums which cover such topics as making a career change and dealing with workplace bullies; and tools for "career mapping," "career snapshots," and "career benchmarking."

Why should a job board go to all the trouble to make such an adjustment?

> THE ANSWER IS **THE GOLDEN RULE OF TRAFFIC DEVELOPMENT:** *WHAT YOU DO TO ATTRACT THE BEST TALENT WILL ALSO ATTRACT MEDIOCRE TALENT, BUT THE CONVERSE IS NOT TRUE.*

Job boards must avoid the constricted vision of corporate classifieds. Their goal must be to provide a value proposition that resonates with 100 percent of the workforce. With passive prospects as well as active job seekers.

While "a job" remains the goal of both (the active job seeker wants a new one, while the passive prospect wants a better one), the more inclusive and respectful term is "employment." Job boards should re-imagine themselves as employment Web-sites.

To do that successfully, job boards cannot abandon the active job seekers who now hold them in such high regard, but should instead supplement their job search content features and functionality with those resources that will serve the needs and interests of passive prospects. In other words, becoming a careerstead is not a repudiation of a job board's traditional mission of job search, but rather an extension of that mission into new areas that serve others in the workforce. It expands a job board's self-definition and brand without detracting from its heritage.

No less important, that career self-management support will enhance and add texture to a job board's job search support. It is just as useful to a person in transition as it is to someone seeking to advance in their field. Moreover, it is exactly what those in transition say they need.

The respondents to WEDDLE's 2012 Source of Employment Survey were asked which features or services job boards should offer. Almost nine-out-of-ten of these individuals (85.6 percent) were either actively in transition or thinking about making a move. It should come as no surprise, therefore, that the #1 response had to do with job search: "More accurate job agent technology (so you receive jobs that match your specification)."

Three of the next four next responses, however, focused on career self-management. In rank order, they were:

- Assessment instruments that will pinpoint your interests and/or work-related preferences;

- Video profiles of employers and their facilities;

- More in-depth news/information about your career field or industry or business in general;

- Discussion forums for online professional networking.

As this Golden Rules establishes, therefore, developing a job board to attract the best talent – the 84 percent of the population who are not in transition and who, because of their greater numbers, represent a relatively larger source of high performers – will also attract everyone else in the workforce, including active job seekers. Focusing a job board exclusively on job search, on the other hand, offers nothing of value to passive prospects and thus will not attract them.

Equally as important, a job board that attracts visitors from 100 percent of the workforce is a powerful sourcing and recruiting resource for its customers, while one that attracts visitors from only a small segment of the workforce is a resource they can and will do without.

PETER WEDDLE

The Golden Rule of Market Positioning

Purity may make philosophers smile, but it turns off paying customers.

Newspapers missed the online employment services revolution in the 1990s because they misunderstood the true nature of their business. When job boards appeared on the scene in the middle of that decade, they dismissed them first as a fad and then as irrelevant to the publishing industry. Newspaper executives boasted that they had ink in their veins. They believed they were in the print business. They weren't.

Newspapers were in the communications business. As far as employers and job seekers were concerned, their job was to transmit useful employment-related information. The modality of that communication – print or online – was far less important than the efficiency and effectiveness with which the information was conveyed. And, job boards with their Internet-based recruitment advertising offered a premium in both speed and value. They delivered more information more quickly and cheaply than newspapers did with the printed page.

Newspapers' myopia cost them dearly. Because they misunderstood their business model, they were unable to see the online threat. Until it was too late. They let job boards capture the allegiance of both employers and job seekers and saw their recruitment advertising business collapse as a result.

Repeating a Past Mistake

Today, too many job boards are repeating the mistake made by newspapers in the 1990s, but with a twist. They misunderstand the true nature of their business AND they have permitted their competitors to brand them as something they aren't. Both of these situations have the potential to cost them the allegiance of employers and job seekers and as a result, push them into a newspaper-like collapse in their business.

Let's look at each of these two mistakes in a bit more detail.

On the one hand, many individual job boards see themselves as purists. They want to "stick to their knitting" or "stay close to their roots." Job boards began as online recruitment advertising businesses, and the entrepreneurs and executives who run these boards are determined to stay true to that original conception. They're convinced that the foundation of their success is selling job posting subscriptions to employers and offering access to those postings to job seekers, and they will not stray from that business model.

On the other hand, job boards in general have let the representatives and cronies of social media sites put them in a box. They've allowed themselves to be defined as vendors whose value proposition is based purely on job postings AND job postings to be defined as old fashioned and out-of-date. They've stood by while self-aggrandizing pundits have – without empirical data or even rational arguments – put them and the service they provide in the same category as buggy whips and rotary phones.

> Today, too many job boards are repeating the mistake made by newspapers in the 1990s... .

Similarly, job boards have remained silent while one recruiting conference and publication after another has followed the faddists and misrepresented their capabilities and quality of service to employers and job seekers alike. They've spent millions exhibiting and advertising in these venues and watched their programs and feature stories describe them as one-trick ponies with a trick that no longer appeals to paying customers. Job boards didn't expect a quid pro quo for their investment, but they did deserve fair treatment ... and they seldom got it.

Not surprisingly, the net result of all this manipulative hysteria has been a diminished job board brand. The value of job board themselves and of the services they provide for employers and recruiters and for job seekers and career activists has not been simply debased – it's been firebombed with duplicitous statements and ridicule.

And tragically, job boards have done little to combat this situation. For the most part – and with some notable exceptions – they've allowed themselves to be painted as purists with a service that is wholly inadequate to the times.

The danger in this situation is extreme and compounded by the fact that too many job boards are actually putting themselves into the very same box their competitors have fashioned. They're making the charge of purity a self-fulfilling brand.

Purity as a Self-Fulfilling Brand

In the face of the social media hype, too many

job boards have circled the wagons and adopted a defensive position that actually reinforces the mischaracterization perpetrated by social media mavens. Tragically, they have accepted the purist definition of their capabilities. They have made credible the claims that new developments in recruitment and job search have passed job boards by. In effect, the box they now find themselves in with a growing number of employers and job seekers is one of their own making. They are, in fact, fixed in place because that's what they want to be.

This situation has transformed the perception of the online employment services industry into one increasingly seen as comprised of two separate and distinct stovepipes of service:

- Social media sites offering state-of-the-art social recruiting

    and

- Job boards offering old-fashioned online recruitment advertising.

What's the impact of this bifurcation on employers and recruiters? It creates a false choice. It sets up an antagonistic relationship between what are nothing more than different but completely compatible and often mutually supportive methods of sourcing and recruiting talent.

Even more troubling, it implies that employers and recruiters have no choice but to pick one or the other. And, far too often, that's exactly what they're doing.

Despite the overwhelming support for job boards in both the CareerXroad's Source of Hire Survey and the WEDDLE's Source of Employment Survey, they're following the lead of social media advocates and consultants and buying into the either-or paradigm.

Here's how one recruiter put it on Bloomberg BusinessWeek on December 13, 2012:

> *In his more than 15 years as a headhunter, Jeff Vijungco has tried Monster (MWW), Craigslist, CareerBuilder, and other online job boards. Lately the head of recruitment at Adobe Systems (ADBE) has scrapped most of them. "I think job postings are such old news," Vijungco says. "Social is the hot new industry."*

And here's how a recruiting consultant frames the situation. It's from Dr. John Sullivan in *The New York Times* on January 28, 2013:

> *Among corporate recruiters, Mr. Sullivan said, random applicants from Internet job sites*

are sometimes referred to as "Homers," after the lackadaisical, doughnut-eating Homer Simpson. The most desirable candidates, nicknamed "purple squirrels" because they are so elusive, usually come recommended.

As harmful as this view of job boards is with employers, the old fashioned label has an even more perverse impact on talent. The best and brightest prospects don't want to hitch their future to sites that are allegedly living in the past so they look elsewhere to advance their careers. And, no matter what they might say in a survey, they want to be seen by and interact with their peers on sites that are reputed to be at the cutting edge in job search so they avoid those that are denigrated by the so-called experts.

In effect, the purity position adopted by at least some job boards makes real the critique their competitors have leveled against the entire industry. They charge – and those sites confirm – that job boards offer limited recruiting services and access to a suboptimal cohort of the talent population. Or, to put it more bluntly, they provide little of value either to employers and recruiters or to the best talent among job seekers and career activists.

Purity as a Pipe Dream

The irony in the purity label becoming a self-fulfilling brand is that, truth be told, job boards were never as pure as they made themselves out to be. In fact, job boards operated by professional societies and associations invented social interaction online. Their listservs, chats and discussion forums appeared as early as the first years of the new millennium and were the forerunners of today's social media sites.

These networking and information sharing features were found in the career centers on sites ranging from the American Institute of Professional Bookkeepers (www.aipb.org) and the Public Relations Society of America (www.prsa.org) to the American Society of Mechanical Engineers (www.asme.org) and the Association for Financial Professionals (www.afponline.org). They may not have been as sleek or sophisticated as today's social media sites, but they were designed to support many of the same activities and did so effectively.

And, they weren't alone. In 2005, *WEDDLE's Guide to Employment Sites on the Internet* started tracking these social platforms on all sites, commercial job boards as well as those operated by professional societies and associations. Of the 350 sites that were profiled that year, over 22 percent reported that they offered a social recruiting capability. By the time the 2011/12 Guide appeared, that number had jumped to 38 percent. And assuming that trend continues apace, a majority of job boards will offer a social capability by late 2015.

Percentage of Job Boards With Social Capability

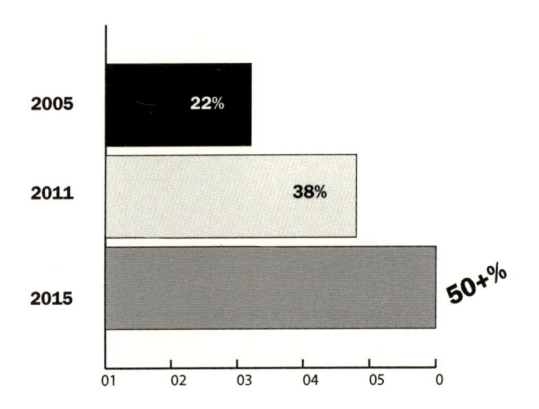

Year	Percentage
2005	22%
2011	38%
2015	50+%

No less important, this social capability has not been limited to the biggest sites or best known brands. For example, if you use the Wayback Machine to revisit 2007 and pull up CareerBoard.com, a site that specializes in local jobs across the U.S., you'll find that it offered not one but two social features in that year: a Job Search Blog and its Ask a Career Coach Q&A. Similarly, a visit to Biospace.com, a site specializing in the life sciences and biotechnology, would reveal not one, but a number of discussion forums open to site visitors in 2007.

And as the table below indicates, this social capability is even more widespread today.

Illustrative Job Board Social Capabilities, 2012

	Blog(s)	Discussion Forum(s)	Message Board(s)	Talent Communities	Q&A
Absolutely Health Care	•	•			
Actuary.com		•			
America's Job Exchange	•				
BenefitsLink.com			•		•
College Recruiter.com	•				
CoolWorks.com		•			
Dice	•	•		•	
MeetingJobs.com	•				

Not only are job boards not as pure as they thought they were, they are much more social than they give themselves credit for. Many sites offer a way for job seekers to interact with one another in their field, in the job market or both and a way for employers and recruiters to engage those professionals and solicit their interest in employment opportunities. Admittedly, this capability isn't always well promoted, but it does in fact exist and provides essentially the same social experience as that now touted by social media sites.

Recapturing the Market Advantage

As noted earlier, a large and growing number of job boards are moving even more aggressively into the social side of recruitment. These multi-featured employment sites offer both traditional recruitment advertising services AND an expanding array of social features. As a result, the social media-promoted view of the job market as a choice between two separate and distinct stovepipes is both out-of-date and inaccurate. Today, job boards are hybrids or more descriptively, "employment sites" and should brand themselves that way in the recruitment marketplace.

A broad cross-section of job boards-turned-employment-sites reveals that this transformation involves three aspects of site design and operation:

- Content Scope
- Relationship Building
- Candidate Acquisition.

The 3 Key Aspects of an Employment Site

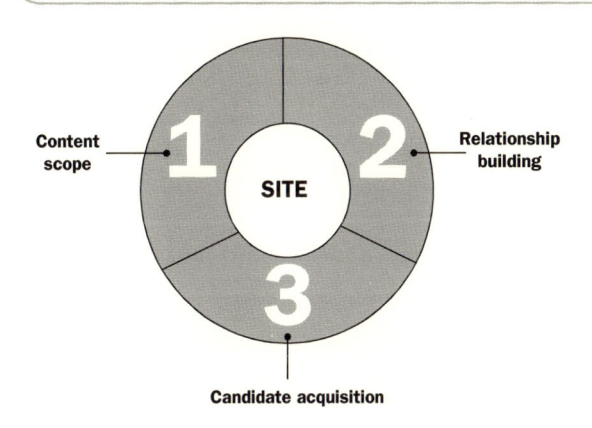

1. Content scope
2. Relationship building
3. Candidate acquisition

SITE

The right kind of development in these three areas transforms a job board into a *talent engagement platform* – one that has the ability to attract high caliber visitors (the same passive, top performers social media sites claim to represent) and provide them with a qualitatively superior experience online so they will return repeatedly and thus enable employers and recruiters to connect with them effectively and efficiently.

Content Scope

Given that passive, high caliber talent is often employed, a growing number of job boards are redesigning their content so that it appeals to people who aren't (actively) looking for a job as well as those who are. In essence, they are expanding their value proposition from job search to career advancement (which includes job search). As a result, they attract a broader cross-section of the workforce to their site and hold their allegiance regardless of their employment status.

For example, JournalismJobs.com provides news and commentary on key topics of interest to journalists as well as the traditional job search information found on most job boards. It has positioned itself as a virtual "career desk" – a one-stop source of information for those who want to stay up-to-date on developments in their field. Whether they work at newspapers, wire services, TV or radio stations, magazines or in online media, reporters, editors, staff writers and their managers can use the site as a key ally in managing their careers successfully.

AuntMinnie.com, a site for radiologists, takes a different tack, focusing on educational content. It provides programs that are so highly regarded, eleven teaching hospitals around the country actually require their new residents to register with the site and participate in a feature called Case of the Day™. An "Aunt Minnie" is radiological jargon for a break in a bone that is so obvious, even your Aunt Minnie would see it. The Case of the Day, on the other hand, delivers a daily dose of instruction by presenting a much more challenging diagnostic test for emerging radiologists.

How is such content social? Highly regarded occupational content is the lingua franca of conversations and debates among those in a field, but especially those who seek to excel on-the-job. To facilitate such interaction, a site will also typically offer both communities and discussion forums for its visitors. Hence, they encourage the social interaction to happen around their own virtual water cooler. And, all the while, those job seekers are just around the corner from the career advancement opportunities posted on the site.

In addition, job boards are now using social media to increase the visibility and even the accessibility of such content among passive prospects as well as active job seekers. For example, HigherEdJobs.

com uses (a) its Twitter feed (@HigherEdCareers) to alert its 4,000+ followers of important content for career success in academia on its own site and (b) its LinkedIn group (HigherEdJobs) to publish content on career topics for its 21,000+ members, which is then linked back to the Author in Residence blog (a book club for educators) as well as the career resources and job postings on its site.

Relationship Building

Top talent can only be recruited if employers are able to persuade them to do the one thing we humans most hate to do: change. Because they are usually employed, they have to be convinced to go from the devil they know (their current employer, boss and commute) to the devil they don't know (a different employer, a new boss and an unfamiliar commute).

Given the significance of that transition (and its inherent risk), many top performers follow a rule first taught to them by their mother. What was that cautionary axiom? "Don't speak to strangers." In most cases, they will only consider a new employment opportunity if it is presented by someone they know.

To recruit top prospects, therefore, recruiters must first get to know them. And – equally if not more important – they must give those prospects a way to get comfortable with them, as well. In short, recruiters must build mutual familiarity and trust, the two pillars of a successful relationship, and do so quickly.

Now, anyone who has ever been in a relationship quickly learns two things: first, they are hard work and second, they take time. For recruiters, that means a commitment to the social experience called networking.

Networking has long been the way that professional relationships are established, and as the word itself indicates, it's netWORK. Historically, old fashioned, face-to-face networking has been a laborious and time-consuming endeavor. For that reason, although recruiters often point to networking as the single most effective way to source top talent, they seldom have the time to practice it

Online networking solves that problem. It is much more efficient than traditional networking and provides not one, but two ways for recruiters to tap the power of relationships.

- Via their participation in online discussion forums which typically focus on key topics of interest among those in a particular field or industry

A growing number of job boards are now either

more aggressively promoting the online discussion forums and listservs they have always offered or are moving to introduce such features on their sites. For example, Dice.com, a site that specializes in IT and engineering, hosts 11 discussion groups on its site. The groups are open to the public and free so they attract strong participation among both active job seekers and passive prospects. They are an effective way for employers and recruiters to build relationships directly with individuals who have specific technical interests and skills.

or

- By alerting them to online discussion forums and other content venues that are likely to be of interest to them and hosted on social media and other sites.

CollegeRecruiter.com has built and now supports a number of candidate communities using Facebook, LinkedIn and Twitter. The site and its principal have 3,000+ friends on Facebook, 4,000+ LinkedIn connections, 13,000 members in its LinkedIn group and 170,000 Twitter followers. It transforms these contacts into relationships by providing them with a steady stream of alerts to relevant content they might otherwise miss. Recruiters can leverage these relationships by participating in the discussions themselves and/or by targeting their job ads to the candidates who are doing so.

> Not only are job boards not as pure as they thought they were, they are much more social than they give themselves credit for.

Regardless of the strategy that's used, however, what's clear is that networking to build relationships is unlike the "cold messaging" that's now typically done on LinkedIn, Facebook and Twitter. The fact that a connection is made on a social media site doesn't change a top prospect's aversion to dealing with a stranger. Therefore, the key to effective social sourcing and recruiting is the acquisition of a new competency. It is the capability to build "blink relationships." Recruiters must now be able to build enough familiarity and trust to get a person to consider changing devils and do so in the blink of an eye.

As this competency is still very much in its infancy, job boards have a short but real window of opportunity to establish themselves as the experts in its principles and practices. By becoming the acknowledged gurus of quickly building genuine relationships online, they differentiate themselves from many social media proponents who treat networking as a "contact sport." In their view, online networking is simply a numbers game; it's all about adding more and more friends or followers or connections on this or that site.

Job boards, in contrast, can brand their approach as a "team sport." It builds meaningful interactions quickly between talented individuals and those seeking to engage, assess and recruit them. That approach brings the definition of online networking much closer to the traditional view of most corporate and third party recruiters. It establishes an alignment of perspectives that will reinforce job boards' own relationship with their customers.

Candidate Acquisition

As noted in the WEDDLE's Source of Employment Survey, one of the reasons that job boards continue to be highly effective recruiting platforms is the caliber of the candidates they deliver. While these individuals are often attracted to the sites by the career-oriented content and networking opportunities they find there, they are also increasingly drawn by the career advancement opportunities which, ironically, job boards are now promoting on conventional social media sites.

For example, Boxwood Technology, a company that designs and powers online career centers for professional societies and associations, has leveraged social media to extend the reach of the recruitment advertising on the sites it supports. Its 1,000+ society and association clients can automatically Tweet their job postings to their followers on Twitter. Equally as important, it has also upgraded the candidate experience on those sites by enabling them to see their LinkedIn connections at an employer once they have applied for an opening there.

In contrast, Dice.com, the IT and engineering employment site, encourages candidates who archive their credentials in its online resume database to add links to their Facebook profile, Twitter account, blog and personal Web-site. That way, when a recruiter finds a candidate of interest, they can immediately begin networking with them online.

In addition, Dice.com will also build a "Talent Network" for employers enabling them to develop a pipeline of both active job seekers and passive prospects and then interact with them, either one-on-one or as a group. In effect, the job board hosts a private social environment for employers which they can use both to advertise their employment opportunities and promote their employment brand.

Similarly, CareerBuilder.com has built talent networks across industries ranging from automotive to work-at-home. They include networks for consortia of employers such as the Texas Dealerships Talent Network, and for individual employers such as the Colonial Life Talent Network and the Sports Authority Talent Network. In addition, the site offers a wide range of consultative services to help employers and recruiters better leverage social media in their recruiting.

In effect, many job boards are now offering a multi-tiered candidate acquisition capability. They feature an employer's jobs on their own sites, leveraging the high caliber traffic they attract with career content and professional networking AND they further feature those jobs on social media sites, leveraging the candidate pools at those sites, as well. And, some expand that tiered approach even further by building private talent pools that give their customers a more exclusive and targeted candidate acquisition capability.

None of these developments are easy or free, so it is entirely appropriate to ask: why should a job board go to all the trouble to rebrand itself as an employment site and remake itself as a talent engagement platform?

> The answer is **the Golden Rule of Market Positioning**: *Purity may make philosophers smile, but it turns off paying customers.*

The days of thinking of job boards and social media sites as separate and distinct recruiting venues are over. Today, there's a more powerful alternative. The hybrid or employment site integrates both recruitment advertising and social media into a comprehensive recruiting solution. It's what job board customers want (and need) and what many job boards are already providing (and should aggressively promote to their customers).

PETER WEDDLE

The Golden Rule of Customer Cultivation

An educated recruiter is your best customer, and an educated job board is the best teacher.

From a job board's perspective, an educated recruiter needs two sets of knowledge:

- Best Strategies – an understanding of the most effective and efficient methods of sourcing and recruiting talent

and

- Best Practices – an understanding of the most productive ways to apply the best strategies for sourcing and recruiting talent.

In a perfect world, every employer and staffing firm would make it their responsibility to ensure that every one of their recruiters has such knowledge and uses it on-the-job. Sadly, we don't live in a perfect world.

Training budgets have been slashed in virtually every enterprise, and that reality leaves job boards with just two options: they can ignore the education of their customers and hope for the best or they can be proactive about developing their customers' expertise and shape the outcome they achieve online. The former is the equivalent of relying on a Ouija board for cultivating customers; the latter is a strategy for managing customer engagement and satisfaction.

Indeed, optimizing the <u>customer</u> experience, to borrow a phrase from recruiters' own playbook, is now a key component of job board success. It is based on ensuring that a site's customers know:

- how to recognize the value a job board delivers and
- how to use job board products and services to their best advantage.

Best Strategies

A study done on the social media practices of corporate recruiters in 2010 came to a startling conclusion. It found that some of the largest and most sophisticated recruiting teams in the U.S. were embarking on the use of social media without any empirical data to justify such a decision.

Among the findings were the following:

- Just 31 percent of the respondents reported that they had seen empirical data addressing social media's effectiveness or efficiency.

- Fewer than half of the respondents (46 percent) said they were measuring the return (in new hires, quality hires or other metrics) on their investment (in financial terms and/or recruiter time) in social media.

and

- An astonishing 79 percent – eight-out-of-ten of the employers – reported that they had NOT done any comparability analysis to assess the relative benefits of social media sites and other methods of sourcing and recruiting, including job boards.

This reality clearly presents job boards with a challenge. Their customers are now making buying decisions without data to confirm the appropriateness of their choices. And, compounding that problem is the fact that those employers that are relying on data for decision-making are more often than not ill-informed. They are being fed bad data.

What's the source of that data?

In most cases, corporate recruiting teams turn to their applicant tracking system (ATS) for data to guide their recruitment investment decisions. And, in far too many cases, their ATS vendors have let them down. To identify the sources of candidates, these companies use simplistic technology (e.g., a drop down window with a list of choices that is often out-of-date, incomplete or both) and the memory of the job seeker. So, what happens? According to a study of 60,000 job seekers done by AllRetailJobs.com, 83 percent – a staggering five-out-of-six candidates – picked the wrong source. And, when their choices were then dutifully reported as valid source data by the ATS vendor, they were perfectly positioned to cause bad strategic decisions by employers.

Job Seekers Who Identified the Wrong Source of Their Knowledge About a Job Opening

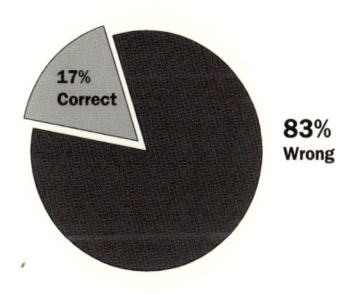

- 17% Correct
- 83% Wrong

But that's not the entirety of the problem. In addition to this data aneurism, there are two additional design flaws in ATS technology:

- First, all too often, the application form that candidates must complete is so lengthy, so complicated or both, it causes a high drop-off rate, especially among top talent. Whether the form's design is the product of the ATS vendor's engineering department or the employer's HR and Legal Departments, the impact is the same: the job board doesn't get credit for delivering prospective new hires that it did, in fact, provide.

- Second, the search functionality for finding applicants once their records are archived in an ATS database can and all too often does miss top prospective hires. Whether this search shortfall is due to the ATS vendor's record parsing technology or the search skills of the employer's recruiters, the impact is, once again, the same: the job board doesn't get credit for delivering prospective new hires that it did, in fact, provide.

> In a perfect world, every employer and staffing firm would make it their responsibility to ensure that every one of their recruiters has such knowledge and uses it on-the-job. Sadly, we don't live in a perfect world.

So, what's to be done?

Despite the decisions of at least some employers to use social media without any empirical justification, there is now a growing interest among employers and recruiters in "big data." Unfortunately, however, there are almost as many definitions for this term as there are experts. Basically, though, it's the use of data – now available on a much more massive scale than ever before – to analyze situations more effectively and make better decisions. In most cases, it involves leveraging today's more powerful technology to support a time-tested axiom of business. In a phrase that's been attributed to both W. Edwards Deming and Peter Drucker, "You can't manage what you don't measure."

Although not yet a universal movement in the recruiting field, this turn toward more metrics and measurement is fast gaining proponents. All functions in the enterprise – from sales and marketing to line operations and IT – are now under considerable pressure to maximize the return on both investments and practices. And data – the bigger, the better – provide both input for making future decisions and a way to monitor those already made.

Moreover, recruiting, as an overhead function, needs that insight and oversight more than most.

This reality presents job boards with a window of opportunity that has two potential upsides:

- It can position job boards to supplant applicant tracking systems as the principal suppliers of credible sourcing data for employers. However, while they can and often already do collect a wealth of data on their product and service outcomes, that data frequently aren't shared with employers on a timely basis.

and

- It can provide a credible and effective way to educate job board customers on the value delivered by their products and services. However, while they certainly have the expertise, job boards will have to leverage their data better to be seen as a trustworthy developmental resource for recruiters and employers.

In effect, the big data phenomenon enables job boards to raise their own standing among employers and recruiters and then to reinforce that position by raising the performance of their customers.

Using Facts to Prove Value

A key question quickly arises when job boards set out to use big data to raise their own standing among employers and recruiters. They must decide which data elements to collect and provide to those customers. There are any number of metrics that can be measured, so it's critical that job boards select the ones that will best enable their customers to evaluate a site's performance accurately. For that – the facts that prove value – should be every job board's ultimate objective. They must educate employers and recruiters on how best to assess their work, so they don't fall prey to the unproven assertions of social media mavens.

To rise to that level, a data element must meet three criteria:

- Employers and recruiters must understand the metric and view it as a credible measure of performance;

- The metric must convey information that they will also view as useful in their decision-making; and

- Job boards must be able to collect, store and transmit the data at a reasonable cost.

Of course, the first metric that comes to mind is candidate quality. In theory, at least, it's a measure of just how good a job board's "output" truly is. And there's the rub. What's the definition of "good?" As important as quality may be, it fails to meet the first criterion listed.

Employers and recruiters have never found a definition of quality on which they all can agree. Is it a candidate's ability to meet a predetermined percentage of an opening's specified requirements and responsibilities? Or, is it their performance on-the-job once they are hired? Is it their propensity to stay with the employer over time? Or, is it their score on a validated test of their skills and knowledge?

There are numerous employers using each of these definitions. Hence, there is no universal standard for quality. Quality is literally in the eyes of the beholder. It is idiosyncratic to each organization. And, this all-over-the-map reality means there is no one data element that job boards (or any other employment site including social media) can collect to measure it.

So, what's the alternative? What metric or metrics will best educate customers and serve job boards' ultimate goal?

The answer is return on investment (ROI). Job

boards should collect data for those metrics that will enable their customers to measure what value they received from the products and services they procured.

While there are other metrics that could be used, the best measures of ROI that meet all three criteria are:

- Views/posting: the number of times a posted ad is opened and viewed by a visitor to a site

and

- Applicants/posting: the number of visitors to a site who apply for a job posted there.

The definition of the first metric is obvious enough. It indicates the number of people who looked at a job posted on the site. The value it is measuring, however, is something else altogether. Views/posting determine just how effective a job board is in attracting the right kind of traffic to its site: active job seekers and passive prospects who may be interested in the employer's open job. While that is clearly not an indication of their qualifications, it is a measure of their preferences. Visitors only look at job postings that interest them. So, matching candidate preferences is the first step in maximizing their propensity to apply. In that sense, therefore, this metric is a valid measure of the ROI an employer or recruiter is able to achieve on the site.

The second metric determines the number of people who click on the email address or the ATS link embedded in a posting (or follow any other instructions the ad provides) to submit their application to the employer. That outcome – a proactive expression of interest from a candidate – is an appropriate measure of return on investment in online recruitment advertising at a job board.

Of course, some will argue that only qualified applicants should be counted, but doing so can misstate a job board's true performance. Why? Because the percentage of qualified applicants is only partially controlled by a job board. As noted in the previous chapter, a job board is certainly responsible for attracting 100 percent of the workforce and thus the best qualified active job seekers and passive prospects. However, employers and recruiters also influence the level of applicant qualifications by their description of the open position. A poorly written job posting or one with a sub-standard value proposition is a sure-fire way to degrade applicant qualifications, even if the site delivers 100 percent of its target candidate pool.

As also previously noted, moreover, applicants/posting does not measure the number of <u>applications</u>

actually received by an employer or recruiter. That number is determined by the total number of applicants delivered by the job board AND by the quality of the experience provided by the employer and/or its applicant tracking system.

For example, according to research conducted by Preptel and reported in *CIO* magazine, "Error-prone applicant tracking systems kill 75 percent of job seekers' chances of landing an interview as soon as they submit their resumes, despite how qualified they may be." Overly long or complicated application forms and other features in many of these systems have transformed the user experience into a nightmare only the most desperate of job seekers will tolerate.

And yet, for many employers, ATS data are all they have to work with when making sourcing decisions. According to the 2012 Global Benchmark Survey conducted by the International Association of Employment Web Sites (IAEWS), the trade organization for the global online employment services industry, more than one-out-of-five job boards (22 percent) don't track views/posting and almost half (47 percent) don't track applicants/posting. For whatever reason, they've let the bad data from applicant tracking systems shape employers' and recruiters' perceptions of their site's value.

Percentage of Job Boards that Do Not Collect Performance Data

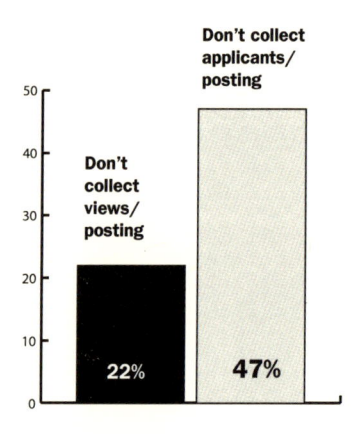

- Don't collect views/posting: **22%**
- Don't collect applicants/posting: **47%**

Further, even among those job boards that do collect such data, many aren't providing it to their customers in an effective and efficient way. Over half of the respondents to the 2012 IAEWS Survey reported that they intended to develop employer dashboards in 2013, which is clearly a step in the right direction. It also means, however, that they haven't been providing such good decision-making data to their customers before now or, at least, not in a timely fashion before now.

In effect, too many job boards are standing by silently while both the non-empirically based opinions of social media mavens and the inaccurate reporting of ATS vendors shape employers' and recruiters' view of their own site's value. That must change. If job boards believe they should be judged on their performance, it is their job to educate their customer on the facts of that performance. And now is the time to begin.

Best Practices

The other body of knowledge and set of skills that result in an educated job board customer is, of course, best practices. Wikipedia defines a best practice as "a method or technique that has consistently shown results superior to those achieved with other means, and that is used as a benchmark." It represents the state-of-the-art in the accomplishment of a task or action. And, while there are a range of such techniques that can be used on a job board, the single most important one by far is the writing of job postings.

Today, unfortunately, most job postings are a modern medical miracle. They are a cure for insomnia in 500 words or less. They may be tolerated by the most desperate of job seekers, but for passive prospects – and especially those who are the most talented and best contributors on-the-job – they are a total turn-off.

Why is this situation occurring? What's behind the malaise in online recruitment advertising?

All too often, corporate and third party recruiters make one or both of two critical mistakes:

- they confuse a job posting with a print classified ad

and/or

- they write their job postings for a generic candidate rather than for top talent.

Let's look at both of these errors in a bit more detail.

THE CLASSIFIED AD ERROR

Print classified ads were job announcements. They evolved during a time when there wasn't a War for Talent, when there were plenty of workers with adequate skills to go around. All employers had to do, therefore, was tell readers that an opening existed and provide information about its requirements and responsibilities. That standard was sufficient to attract enough applicants to ensure the job would be filled relatively quickly and with someone who was relatively qualified to do the work.

Today, however, this kind of job announcement is not sufficient. The War for Talent isn't business jargon or a made-for-marketing slogan. It's real. And, it acknowledges the reality of the "economic singularity."

The term "singularity" was coined by the academician and science fiction writer Vernor Vinge. He used it to designate that point in time when machines would become smarter than humans. Happily, we've not yet crossed that demarcation line.

What, then, is the "economic singularity?" It's a term I coined to denote that point in time when the employees of many companies outside the U.S. become smarter that the employees of many companies in the U.S. And unfortunately, that singularity is a demarcation line we have, in fact, already passed. Whether they operate in global, domestic or even local markets, American employers are no longer competing against companies with cheaper labor; they're competing against companies with smarter labor – workers with the latest education and up-to-date skills in the occupations required by a modern economy.

> If job boards believe they should be judged on their performance, it is their job to educate their customer on the facts of that performance. And now is the time to begin.

This shift in the competitive dynamic has upped the performance requirements for all workers – it has increased demand at the very same time the supply of those who can meet the requirements has shrunk. As a consequence, there are now significant shortages of both high performing workers and those with critical skills. The resulting competition for such candidates is intense and will remain so for years to come. And, job postings must evolve to meet that challenge.

To be effective in today's highly competitive market for talent, job postings must be viewed not as announcements (or their corporate kissing cousins, position descriptions) but as *electronic sales brochures*. They must sell talented workers as well as in-form them. Indeed, as noted in an earlier chapter, they must have the persuasive power to convince candidates to change devils – to go from their current employer, boss and commute to a new employer, a different boss and a changed commute.

THE GENERIC CANDIDATE ERROR

Equally as important, job postings must no longer be written for a generic candidate. Such ads lump all job seekers together and don't recognize or accommodate the important differences between active job seekers and passive prospects and between top performers and also-rans. As a result, they focus entirely on the requirements and responsibilities of a job – they provide the information employers want all job seekers to know.

While that approach makes writing a job posting much easier, it violates a principal tenet of good sales. To engage and convince a customer to buy (in this case an organization's value proposition as an employer), the seller has to put themselves in the buyer's shoes. Which begs the question: who are the buyers? Who are employers trying to recruit – any job seeker or the best talent?

As the answer is almost always the best talent (hard as it is to believe, there are still some employers who say they don't want to hire top performers because it will cost too much), a job posting must be written for that population and address its unique attributes and needs. And, the best talent thinks requirements and responsibilities are words only an employer could love. They aren't looking for a job, even when they are in transition. As noted earlier, however, they are almost always on the lookout for a career advancement opportunity.

How is a job posting transformed into the description of such a value proposition?

According to research conducted by the Recruiting Round Table, the best talent must be motivated to respond by two very specific kinds of triggers. The first has to do with focus: they expect the ad to focus on them, on what they want to know, not on what the employer wants them to know.

To be effective, therefore, a job posting must translate an opening's requirements and responsibilities into the answers to the five key questions that matter most to top talent:

> What will they get to do?

> What will they get to learn?

> What will they get to accomplish?

> With whom will they get to work?

> How will they be recognized and rewarded?

The second trigger has to do with effect: top talent expect a job posting to be persuasive. They aren't desperate for work, so informing them about an opening isn't sufficient to influence their behavior. To activate them, a job posting must convince them that the entire employment experience is extraordinary. The job AND the employer together must present a situation that is so special and potentially advantageous to them, they can't afford to pass it up. Said another way, the ad must position the employer as a career advancement provider and the opening as a career advancement opportunity.

Just as there are five questions an ad must answer to position a job as a career advancement opportunity, there are five questions it must address to position an employer as a career advancement provider. They are:

> How does it support employees and enable them to do their best work?

> How does it communicate with employees and keep them informed?

> What priority does it give to employee development and how is it provided?

> What is its track record (i.e., is it serving its customers well and will it continue to do so)?

> What are the vision and values of its leaders (i.e., is its mission important and respected)?

The Skills Gap Among Recruiters

Far too many recruiters today don't know how to write an electronic sales brochure or are prevented from doing so. They've never been taught how to use the written word to "sell" a reluctant person of talent on the value proposition of their opening. Or, they work for an employer that has so reduced the size of the recruiting team that they simply don't have the time to develop an effective ad. And, in the worst of all cases, they have neither the skills nor the time to do what's required.

How has this situation come to be?

There is undoubtedly a host of contributing factors, but the most important has been the shortsighted behavior of too many corporate leaders. These executives go on cable business shows or sit for interviews with business publications and proclaim the importance of talent in today's global marketplace, and then they return to their corner offices and slash the staffing, budget and priority of their recruiting teams. Instead of using the slower pace of recruiting during the last recession to build up the skills and knowledge of in-house recruiters, they laid them off. They lost a generation of job posting expertise in the process.

Compounding this situation was the myopia

of many of today's commercial recruitment conferences. Instead of providing a well-round curriculum that addressed all facets of a recruiter's required skills and knowledge – including the best practices in writing a job posting – they hopped on the social media bandwagon and provided programs that were almost entirely devoted to LinkedIn, Twitter and Facebook (with an occasional session on mobile recruiting thrown in for spice).

What's happened as a result?

Not surprisingly, most poorly written job postings perform poorly. Some generate nothing but the sound of silence from potential applicants. Others attract a host of applications from people who should never have applied. In either case, employers and recruiters don't blame the job posting for such an unsatisfactory ROI. They blame the job board.

In their view, it was the site which didn't produce. And sadly, as inappropriate and harmful as that view may be, it frequently doesn't end there. Once a job board under-performs thanks to a poorly written job posting, the dissatisfied customers use their social media connections to spread the bad news. The modern medical miracle metastasizes into a life threatening disease for the job board.

What's the Cure?

Job boards must not make the same mistake that newspapers made with their customers. Print recruitment ads were often just as poorly written as job postings are today, yet newspapers decided it was beneath their dignity to educate employers and recruiters on how best to write them. Recruitment advertising agencies then filled the resulting vacuum, effectively severing the relationship between newspapers and their customers. As a result, the agencies became the partners that employers and recruiters needed in their recruitment advertising campaigns, while newspapers devolved into nothing more than order takers.

How can job boards avoid this outcome?

THE ANSWER IS THE **GOLDEN RULE OF CUSTOMER CULTIVATION:** *AN EDUCATED RECRUITER IS YOUR BEST CUSTOMER, AND AN EDUCATED JOB BOARD IS THE BEST TEACHER.*

Job boards must assume the role of educating recruiters and employers on the best practices of online recruitment advertising and make doing so a priority.

This educational outreach should be directed at the widest possible audience and include both a job board's current and potential customers and even the general recruiter population, rather than some narrow subset of its "best customers." It should be delivered in multiple media, using Webinars, video tutorials, print collateral, classroom presentations, users' group meetings and other formats, rather than a single distribution channel. And, it should be delivered continuously, with regular updates and refresher programs, rather than as a one-off, check-mark-in-the-done-box initiative.

Equally as important, the instruction should cover both best strategies and best practices.

- Assuming a job board has committed itself to collecting and delivering performance data, its training program should connect the dots between a recruiting team's fiduciary responsibility to invest its organization's money wisely and the power of empirically-based decision-making. It should educate recruiters and employers on the metrics that can help them optimize their ROI in recruitment advertising and show them how it provides such data for that purpose.

- Assuming a job board has kept itself up-to-date on the state-of-the-art in online recruitment advertising, the training should also connect the dots between the core competencies required for a recruiting team to wage and win the War for Talent and the power of persuasively written online job ads. It should cover the format, content, voice, vocabulary and other key facets involved in the writing of effective electronic sales brochures.

The goal of this effort is two-fold. First and most importantly, it is to educate a job board's customer base so they make best use of the products and services it offers and thus become satisfied and repeat customers. Second, it is to rebrand job boards so they are no longer seen as simply subscription order takers but rather as talent acquisition partners who are dedicated to their customers' success.

PETER WEDDLE

The Golden Rule of Customer Satisfaction

One trick ponies may thrive in the circus, but they're doomed to extinction in the marketplace.

It's common for the owners and operators of job boards to think that they are in the job posting business. After all, that's the service they've been selling to employers and recruiters since they came online in the mid-1990s. Moreover, the view seems to reflect a reasonable progression in the natural order of things:

- recruitment communications began with handwritten Help Wanted signs posted in shop windows;

- then they progressed to classified ads that provided some job information but were visible for only a single day and were relatively expensive;

- until finally the Internet revolution created online job postings that could be as detailed as an employer wanted to make them, stayed in circulation for 30 days or more and were relatively cheap.

As history went, it just made good sense ... except for one thing. The progression didn't stop there. While job postings were clearly an advance over the recruitment tools used by employers and recruiters in the early and mid 20th century, their needs continued to evolve in the 21st century. The situation facing employers and recruiters today is vastly different from that which they faced in the previous millennium. And, this new reality leaves job boards with just one option: they too must progress in order to keep up.

That's easier said than done, of course. Companies aren't people, but they are human institutions. They reflect the attributes of their leaders and employees. For job boards – indeed, for any enterprise – that means change is hard. Just as we humans are uncomfortable with the risk, disruption and unknowns of doing something different, so too are the enterprises we run. As a consequence, at least some job boards see the changing marketplace – they recognize the evolving needs of their customers – but they refuse to adjust.

The Roots of the Business

As previously noted, in the late 1990s, the U.S. and worldwide economy was expanding so rapidly that a War for Talent erupted. Companies were battling to hire hundreds, even thousands of new workers, and the skills they needed were the skills most Americans had or could acquire relatively quickly. In essence, this first theatre in the War for Talent was a quantitative rather than a qualitative competition. It was a War for Any Talent.

The strategy most employers and recruiters used in this environment was a departure from what had normally been done in the past: they relied on a new sourcing method to connect with candidates and then used incentives to sell the value proposition of their openings. For the first time ever:

- they opted for job postings rather than (or sometimes in addition to) classified ads to promote their openings

and

- they offered come-ons ranging from hiring bonuses to expensive give-aways to lure talent in the door.

There were countless news reports of employers and recruiters flocking to Monster.com, CareerBuilder.com, HeadHunter.net and a growing number of smaller sites to post their jobs and courting even recent college graduates with BMWs and all-expense paid vacations to exotic destinations.

Better than eight-out-of-ten (81 percent) of the employers and recruiters that responded to WEDDLE's 1999 Source of Employment Survey said they had posted a job on a commercial job board. Almost half (49 percent) had posted a job on a job board operated by an association, alumni or other affinity group. And, better than one-in-three (38 percent) had purchased a print classified ad which included a job posting on the publication's Web-site.

> **Employers & Recruiters Using Job Postings in 1999**

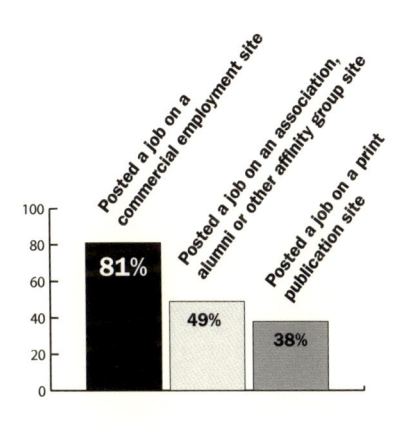

- Posted a job on a commercial employment site: **81%**
- Posted a job on an association, alumni or other affinity group site: **49%**
- Posted a job on a print publication site: **38%**

The logic behind this shift to job postings was simple and straight forward. Employers and recruiters were simply following the breadcrumb trail left by job seekers. Those transitioning workers didn't have all that many options, so while many continued to use traditional job search tools – checking the newspaper classifieds and sending their resume into an employer by postal mail – more and more of them were also venturing out onto the Internet. Indeed, 72 percent of the job seekers who responded to WEDDLE's 1999 Source of Employment Survey reported that they had searched the job database on a commercial employment site, while 43 percent said they had archived their resume in the database there.

Job postings were a novel and effective weapon for waging the War for Any Talent. They put employment opportunities in front of millions of people who had the skills and knowledge to do the work. And, in significant numbers, those individuals applied for the openings. When the employers and recruiters who responded to WEDDLE's 1999 Survey were asked how helpful their online recruitment advertising had been, 60 percent said Very Helpful. Just 7.1 percent described it as "No more helpful than other recruitment methods."

The New Talent Battlefield

Battlefields are highly dynamic environments, and the battlefield known as the job market is no exception. Indeed, that battlefield changed dramatically in the first decade of the current millennium. The War for Talent morphed from a quantitative to a qualitative competition. It was no longer a War for Any Talent; it had become a War for the Best Talent.

The pace of technological development greatly

accelerated, significantly changing the skills required in traditional occupations and creating entirely new ones. In addition, overseas competitors emerged in both domestic and global markets, and, as noted earlier, they often employed workers who had the very latest knowledge and skills in their occupations. As a consequence, employers and recruiters no longer needed more workers, they needed better ones. They were (and still are) in the market for workers who could excel on-the-job.

> The situation facing employers and recruiters today is vastly different from that which they faced in the previous millennium. And, this new reality leaves job boards with just one option: they too must progress in order to keep up.

At the same time, a plethora of new communications channels emerged. Job seekers could now conduct their job search using any or all of a range of media, platforms and venues. Whether it was LinkedIn, Twitter or Facebook, general purpose or niche job boards, search engines or aggregators, their desktop computer or the cloud, their laptop computer or their smart phone, they could be anywhere at any time on any of a host of devices.

The options are numerous and becoming more so, which inevitably splinters the workforce into smaller and smaller cohorts. As a consequence, no one medium, Web-site or platform can provide the scale necessary to be used exclusively or even with a limited number of other channels to wage the War for the Best Talent, at least, not if the goal is victory. Why? Because victory is now defined as an organization's success in capturing more than its fair share of those with rare skills and those who are top performers.

This unlimited array of limited options creates an entirely new talent acquisition ecosystem for employers and recruiters ... and by extension for job boards, as well. Although some have characterized this development as a rejection of job postings, nothing could be further from the truth. As noted earlier, employers and recruiters continue to see great value in online recruitment advertising.

Further, when respondents to WEDDLE's 2012

Source of Employment Survey were asked to rate the quality of candidates sourced online, 36 percent described them as "among our best employees" and 42 percent said they were "above average employees." And, when those same respondents were asked to evaluate the diversity of candidates generated by online recruitment advertising, almost six-out-of-ten (59.2 percent) said it was excellent or above average.

Employer & Recruiter Rating of Job Board Candidate Quality

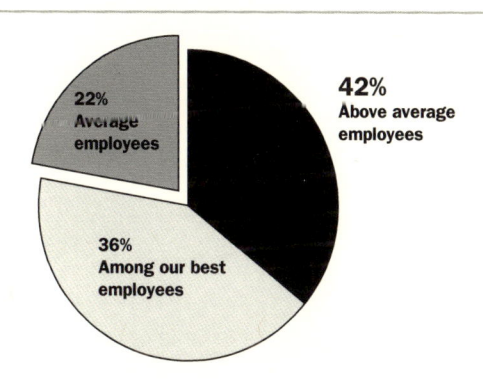

- 42% Above average employees
- 36% Among our best employees
- 22% Average employees

Unlike the situation with newspapers, then, the new talent ecosystem doesn't indicate a flight from job boards, but rather a continuation of employers' and recruiters' efforts to follow the breadcrumb trail left by job seekers in general and the best talent in particular.

What does this new talent acquisition ecosystem look like?

The new talent acquisition ecosystem encompasses the full (and still evolving) array of strategies, tactics, technologies and applications that can be used to acquire top talent online and off. It is specific products and services as well as the more complex and multifaceted capabilities that are possible with their effective integration. It includes everything from mobile apps for job alert transmission to job postings with embedded video, from data mining and social sourcing to talent network formation and communication, from corporate Web-site design and development to e-staffing and e-executive search services.

As unsettling as this vast new tableau may be – it is, to be sure, the expression of change on steroids – it also offers job boards a pathway to transformation. It enables them to select from a more expansive array of capabilities to introduce their own more powerful set of products and services for their customers. That more fulsome capability, in turn, repositions them in the market and expands their revenue potential. It enables job boards to both brand themselves and operate as *talent acquisition centers of excellence* rather than as job posting vendors.

MARKET REPOSITIONING

Wikipedia defines a center of excellence as "an entity that provides leadership, evangelization, best practices, research, support and/or training for a focus area." A talent acquisition center of excellence, therefore is an organization which has the knowledge and skills to provide leadership, evangelization, best practices, research, support and/or training in the full array of modern sourcing and recruiting tools, techniques, technology, applications, strategies and tactics required to win the War for the Best Talent.

It may not – indeed probably will not – offer all of these products and services itself, but it knows their strengths and weakness and how best to tailor a self-selected subset of them into an integrated solution for each of its customers. No less important, it delivers that expertise as a trusted partner of each organization, providing consultation and support as well as the products and services within its own portfolio.

Does that mean job boards should no longer focus on job posting sales? Of course not. Selling, whether it's done by automation, telephone or in-person sales calls will obviously continue to be important, but it must now be transacted within the frame of a larger relationship. That larger frame must give the customer the sense that they are working with – not buying from – an expert in talent acquisition who is committed to helping them develop a tailored, comprehensive, and cost-effective campaign for recruitment.

The best analog to this transformative shift is the product and service ecosystems now being created by technology companies. Brands from Apple and Microsoft to Google and Facebook no longer believe that a single core product – whether it's the world's most prevalent operating system or the world's dominant search engine – can sustain a business. As a result, they are pushing out the boundaries of what they offer to their customers. They are moving from a one-trick pony to a thoroughbred with a range of capabilities. Instead of offering a single product or service, they are now offering a multifaceted solution.

For example, Apple doesn't just sell computers, tablets and phones any more. It supplements that hardware business with an operating system, core apps and an online entertainment services enterprise. The net result is not only more revenue, it's more loyal customers as well. And the source of that loyalty?

The ability of each customer to pick and choose from an array of products and services to tailor an experience that is right for and unique to them.

Similarly, Microsoft has supplemented its core operating system product with a range of new hardware. It recently unveiled its first computer, and the bet is that it will shortly introduce a smart phone, as well. Meanwhile, Google has extended its search business with its Nexus brand of smart phones and tablets, and almost certainly has even more products and services in the pipeline. Its recent acquisition of Motorola Mobility, for example, suggests it will be launching new software services for its Android mobile technology.

REVENUE POTENTIAL

The new and more expansive talent acquisition ecosystem also offers job boards a significant upside in terms of potential revenue growth. While the extent of that growth will clearly be influenced by an organization's strategy and tactics, operational excellence and leadership, it is first and foremost a function of the size of the market in which it competes. And, the market for a broad array of talent acquisition services is significantly larger than that for job postings.

While there are numerous estimates for the exact size of the job posting market, there is no doubt about its general order of magnitude. Indeed, virtually every credible estimate concludes that the total market is well below $10 billion annually.

For example, BMO Capital Markets Corporation estimates that the U.S. market for job postings was $5.3 billion in 2011. Although it forecasts a healthy compounded annual growth rate of 4 percent between that year and 2015, the growth will only bring the total market to just over $6 billion in that year.

In contrast, according to the American Staffing Association, the U.S. marketplace for staffing services – an imperfect but nevertheless instructive analog for an expansive talent acquisition ecosystem – was $109.5 billion in 2011. The global staffing market in that year was four times larger. Staffing Industry Analysts calculated that it was $406 billion, with the U.S. market the largest in volume followed by the market in Europe.

Now clearly, job boards are not going to become staffing firms. They can, however, compete with staffing firms for a significant segment of their market. And, when they do – when they adopt a more expansive view of their business model – their revenue potential will increase by a factor of 20 or more.

Instead of competing in an annual market of barely more than $5 billion in the U.S., they will be competing in a market of over $100 billion.

The Choice That's No Choice At All

In theory, at least, job boards have a choice. They can either embrace the new talent acquisition ecosystem or they can ignore it. They can "stick close to home" and continue to offer comfortably familiar job posting services – from one-off sales to subscriptions, from featured ad positioning to banners and buttons – or they can go through the challenges of change and introduce a broader array of capabilities that leverage new technologies and ideas.

While the culture and leadership of individual job boards will have an impact on that decision, the customer also gets a vote. And, their vote counts most, at least if the goal is to create a sustainable and profitable business. No less important, their view on this matter has been made crystal clear.

Each year, the IAEWS holds two conferences for its members and at each event, a senior recruiting executive is invited to present the closing keynote. We ask them to give the attendees their unvarnished and candid assessment of the performance of job boards and their wish list of changes and improvements they would like to see from the job board community. For the past five years, every executive, whether they worked for a Fortune 500 company or a technology start-up being lionized in the business press, offered a variation on the same theme: *We'd like to see job boards stop selling us job posting subscriptions and start offering us talent acquisition solutions.* In effect, they were asking job boards to adapt to the new talent acquisition ecosystem and operate as a center of excellence.

> The new and more expansive talent acquisition ecosystem also offers job boards a significant upside in terms of potential revenue growth.

Similarly, WEDDLE's 2012 Source of Employment Survey asked employers and recruiters to identify which capabilities job boards should add to their portfolio. While they could indicate "None," the top two selections, accounting for 50 percent of the responses, were "Staffing firm-like services (e.g., a slate of 8-10 best qualified applicants)" and "Aggregator-like services (e.g., job posting to other job boards)." In contrast, variations on traditional job posting services – such things as "alternative job posting formats" or "Featured positioning of job postings" each attracted just 11 percent of the responses.

When the survey asked respondents to identify which additional services they would be willing to pay for at a job board, the top two selections, again accounting for more than 50 percent of the responses, were "Better matching technology for candidate-to-position and/or candidate-to-organizational culture" and "Job ad distribution to social media/social networking sites." Once again, job board customers were asking job boards to get out of their traditional and narrowly defined role and become more of a partner in solving their talent acquisition needs.

In the end, the choice facing job boards in the new talent acquisition ecosystem is no choice at all. Why?

> THE ANSWER IS THE **GOLDEN RULE OF CUSTOMER SATISFACTION**: *ONE TRICK PONIES MAY THRIVE IN THE CIRCUS, BUT THEY'RE DOOMED TO EXTINCTION IN THE MARKETPLACE.*

Job boards must re-imagine themselves as talent acquisition centers of excellence that provide:

- expertise in a broad array of talent acquisition capabilities

and

- tailored solutions that draw on that expertise for their customers.

And, once that capability is in place, they must brand themselves and operate accordingly. That's the only way to win in the 21st century employment services marketplace. The definition of what it takes to satisfy customers today is different than it was when job boards first came into being, and adapting to that new reality is now a precondition for success.

About the International Association of Employment Web Sites

The International Association of Employment Web Sites is the trade organization for the global online employment services industry. Its Members include job boards, career portals, aggregators, job ad distribution companies, recruitment advertising agencies and the vendors which support them. Collectively, they power or operate over 60,000 sites worldwide.

For more information, please visit www.EmploymentWebSites.org.

PETER WEDDLE

WEDDLE's Syndicated Content for Job Boards

Peter Weddle has written a biweekly column about Recruiting Best Practices for the interactive edition of *The Wall Street Journal* and *The New York Times* and a similar column on Job Search Best Practices for CNN.com. In addition, he has written or edited over two dozen books on the changing world of work and the keys to success in the 21st century.

All of that experience is the foundation for three biweekly syndicated columns which employment sites can now license for distribution to their employer and recruiter customers and job seeker and career activist visitors. Each column is new and original content that delivers both the principles and the practices required for success.

The three columns are:

- WEDDLE's Column on Best Practices in online sourcing and recruiting.
- WEDDLE's Column on Best Practices in online and traditional job search.
- WEDDLE's Column on Best Practices in career self-management and success.

For additional information on how you can bring this unique content to your site's customers and visitors, contact WEDDLE's at 203.964.1888 or peter@weddles.com.

About the Author

Described by *The Washington Post* as "a man filled with ingenious ideas," Peter Weddle has authored or edited over two dozen books and been a columnist for *The Wall Street Journal, National Business Employment Weekly* and CNN.com.

Weddle is also the CEO of WEDDLE's Research & Publishing, which specializes in employment and workforce issues, and the Managing Director of the International Association of Employment Web Sites, the trade organization for the global online employment services industry.

His most recent books include *A Multitude of Hope: A Novel About Rediscovering the American Dream*; *The Career Fitness Workbook: How to Find, Win & Hang Onto the Job of Your Dreams*; *The Career Activist Republic* and *The Success Matrix: Wisdom *from the Web on How to Get Hired & Not Be Fired.*

An Airborne Ranger, Weddle is a graduate of the United States Military Academy at West Point. He has attended Oxford University and holds advanced degrees from Middlebury College and Harvard University.